Career Discovery

Careers If You Like the Outdoors

Stuart A. Kallen

ReferencePoint Press®

San Diego, CA

© 2018 ReferencePoint Press, Inc.
Printed in the United States

For more information, contact:
ReferencePoint Press, Inc.
PO Box 27779
San Diego, CA 92198
www. ReferencePointPress.com

LIBRARY OF CONGRESS CATALOGING-IN-PUBLICATION DATA

Name: Kallen, Stuart A., 1955– author.
Title: Careers If You Like the Outdoors/by Stuart A. Kallen.
Description: San Diego, CA: ReferencePoint Press, Inc., 2018. | Series:
   Career discovery | Includes bibliographical references and index. |
   Audience: Grade 9 to 12.
Identifiers: LCCN 2016045976 (print) | LCCN 2017005617 (ebook) | ISBN
   9781682821404 (hardback) | ISBN 9781682821411 (eBook)
Subjects: LCSH: Vocational guidance—Juvenile literature. | Outdoor
   life–Vocational guidance—Juvenile literature. | Outdoor
   recreation—Vocational guidance—Juvenile literature.
Classification: LCC HF5381.2 .K348 2018 (print) | LCC HF5381.2 (ebook) | DDC
   331.702—dc23
LC record available at https://lccn.loc.gov/2016045976

CONTENTS

Introduction: Air and Sunshine on the Job

If you can't imagine spending your work life sitting in a cubicle and wistfully staring out the window all day, look to the outdoors when choosing a career. Outdoor jobs are available in a number of industries, including construction, agriculture, tourism, environmental science, and the arts. Some outdoor jobs, such as outdoor educator and conservationist, appeal to the ecologically minded and often take place in scenic areas. Other outdoor careers, like vineyard manager, landscape architect, and groundskeeper, are good for those who have a passion for plants and enjoy watching things grow. People who work outdoors as surveyors and environmental scientists have more urban-based careers; they often spend their days along roadways or at abandoned industrial sites. Whatever their position, most people who work outdoors would not trade their job for one that required them to be stuck at a desk all day. As wilderness therapy field instructor Eric Hanson says, "The physical activity and the time outside involved with [outdoor] jobs makes for a healthy, vibrant lifestyle. . . . You enjoy a work environment that is conducive to thinking and processing your life. . . . You cannot get this kind of connection in an office."[1]

Healthy, Happy Occupations

The link between the great outdoors, a healthy lifestyle, and positive thinking has been discussed by philosophers for centuries. In 1862 naturalist Henry David Thoreau wrote that when we spend time outdoors, "there will be so much the more air and sunshine in our thoughts."[2] While Thoreau was more of a philosopher than a scientist, recent research proves that being outside contributes to health and happiness. According to a 2016 study at Chiba University in Japan, those who spend time outdoors are less likely to experience anxiety, depression, and health problems like high blood pressure, heart disease, and obesity. Conversely, many who work indoors are exposed to health hazards. In 2011 the US Environmental Protection Agency (EPA) released a report warning of a condition called sick building syndrome. The syndrome, caused by toxic building materials, mold, and stale air in ventilation systems, can trigger a host of allergy-like symptoms. The EPA said circulated office air can be up to one hundred times dirtier than outdoor air and that around one-third of all Americans work in sick buildings.

Enjoy Your Job

Whether they perform their jobs indoors or out, most adults spend half their waking hours at work. So if you're planning an outdoor career, it's important to figure out what kind of work you'll truly enjoy. There are pros and cons to every job. For example, people who work as farmers and horticulturists spend their days shaping the natural landscape, growing food for thousands of people, or simply making a park or backyard a more beautiful place. If you like working with tools and want a job that does not require long hours in front of a computer, a career in agriculture might be for you. However, this type of work can be seasonal; those who live in a cold, rainy climate might be unemployed for months at a stretch. Agricultural work can also be dangerous and hard on the body; hoisting bags of soil, working with power tools, and driving heavy equipment for many hours every day can be a tough way to earn a living.

Then there are those who value adventure over a fat bank account. Marine biologists, for example, don't earn large salaries but spend their time diving, boating, and studying fish and other marine creatures. There's also plenty of excitement in the lives of park rangers, whose "office" consists of backcountry trails, wildlife habitats, and stunning scenery. If you can see yourself getting paid to kayak, climb mountains, fish, and ride horses, adventure tour guide jobs are out there waiting to be filled.

Most people who work outdoors will never earn as much as number crunchers, engineers, and information technology (IT) geeks, but their jobs provide a kind of satisfaction that can't be found under florescent lights. As naturalist John Muir once said, "Thousands of tired, nerve-shaken, over civilized people are beginning to find out that going [outdoors] is going home."[3] Since most people spend eight hours or more every day at their jobs, and being outside is like "going home," working outdoors might be the best way to earn a living—while living as you earn.

Farmer

Walk into a grocery store and look around. The basic ingredients in every edible item on display, from the nastiest junk food to the most wholesome organic salad, originated on a farm. In the United States, farmers provide breakfast, lunch, and dinner to over 324 million people every day. In addition, about one-third of all US farm products are exported to other countries to help feed people around the globe.

Feeding the world is a big business; America's 2.2 million farmers bring in $500 billion annually. Nearly 96 percent of farms are family owned. In agricultural states like Nebraska and Iowa, for example, it is not unusual to meet people who are sixth-generation farmers. And nearly nine out of ten agricultural families own small farms, around 250 acres (101 ha) in size. About 4 percent of farmers have large holdings of over 2,000 acres (809 ha). In many cases a farmer's skills and technical expertise have come from a heritage of farming passed down from parents, grandparents, and even great-grandparents.

What Do Farmers Do?

Farmers grow crops; raise chickens, turkeys, pigs, cows, and other livestock;

and produce milk, cheese, and other dairy products. Farmers often work from sunup to sundown planting seeds, fertilizing plants, eliminating weeds and insects, harvesting crops, and handling livestock. To be successful, farmers must be knowledgeable about a range of things, from soil conditions to plant and animal diseases. They also need to know how to repair and maintain machinery and farm infrastructure, such as irrigation systems, sewers, buildings, fences, and animal shelters. And all this must be done while keeping an eye on the unpredictable weather, which can bring profits or pain.

Farming is about more than fixing, planting, and growing, however; it is also a tough business that demands a strong understanding of agricultural economics. Farmers spend large sums to purchase fuel, seeds, agricultural chemicals, livestock, and large complex machinery. Oftentimes this is done with money borrowed from a bank or government agency. Farmers also act as their own sales agents for crops, dairy products, and livestock, monitoring the constantly fluctuating prices of these commodities. This means farmers must always hedge their bets against the market, planting a mix of crops that will ensure a profit even if the price of one or more crops declines. Additionally, farmers must navigate complex programs, such as crop insurance and federal farm subsidies, which can provide a monetary cushion when times are bad. And like any small business owner, farmers are required to keep financial and tax records and follow state and federal employment regulations when hiring and firing workers.

The job requires analytical thinkers who can constantly monitor their land and livestock with accuracy and precision. Farmers need to make hard decisions based on thoughtful analysis while also reacting to external forces like market conditions and weather. Modern farmers need strong mechanical skills to operate, maintain, and repair large machines like combines, cultivators, tractors, trucks, and conveyors. Farmers also deal with smaller equipment, such as milk machines, grain grinders, and chain saws. While farmers may do a lot of physical work, they must also be good thinkers. A thorough knowledge of agricultural software is vital in the computer age. Programs like Conservis give a farmer control over planning, purchasing, planting, harvesting, marketing, and keeping inventory. Basic educational tools are also put to the test every day. As Illinois farmer Keith Jolley explains, there is a lot of math used in farming:

> You have to able to use different areas of mathematics, such as weights and measures, addition, subtraction, multiplication, division, rates and ratios, geometry and area, interest rates, and taxes. . . . We also use mathematics when deciding what to plant and when to sell. We watch the prices. It is kind of strange. If it rains in Brazil, then the price of beans drops. It takes something really good to happen to make the prices go up. But that's farming![4]

How Do You Become a Farmer?

If you love the outdoors, like to work with animals, and take satisfaction from growing and harvesting plants, you might consider farming as a career choice. You can start while you're still in high school by volunteering at a local farm or joining a student organization like Future Farmers of America, which provides an education in agriculture to its members.

Many farmers get by with only a high school education, but since the agricultural business has grown more complicated, many obtain associate's or bachelor's degrees in agriculture or related fields. The government encourages farmers to seek education, and most state university systems have one or more land-grant college with a school of agriculture. These schools teach courses in agriculture business and economics, plant and animal breeding, dairy science, and farm management.

College graduates can gain farming experience through universities and government agencies that offer work programs to prospective farmers. For example, the Beginning Farmer and Rancher Development Program (BFRDP) finances a mentor program to connect recent agriculture grads with experienced farm-

Hard Work and a Clear Mind

"During my stint [as an apprentice in upstate New York] at Hill Hollow Farm, I often wanted to throw in the towel, when farm work seemed like sheer drudgery, tedious tasks stretching out to infinity. . . . My sunburnt skin took the shade of a country ham. . . . I had to muck out the deep crust of [manure] from a sweltering pig barn. Sheer force of will kept my breakfast down. And yet—I felt great. . . . There was something purifying and warm about all the hard work, something that washed away the static in my head."

—Jesse Hirsch, staff writer at *Modern Farmer*

Jesse Hirsch, "So You Want to Be a Farmer. . . ," *Modern Farmer*, September 15, 2014. http://modernfarmer.com.

ers. When US Department of Agriculture (USDA) deputy secretary Krysta Harden announced a new $18 million funding program for the BFRDP, she said:

> As new farmers and ranchers get started, they are really looking to their community for support. The Beginning Farmer and Rancher Development Program empowers these farmers and ranchers to bring innovative ideas to the table when it comes to addressing food security, creating economic enterprises, and building communities. Programs like these are evidence that an investment in beginning farmers and ranchers is an investment in our future.[5]

Farm Apprenticeships

Even as the world population continues to grow, the number of people entering the agriculture business is declining. Only 6 percent of farmers are under age thirty-five, while about one-quarter are over sixty-five. This means young farmers are in demand. But breaking into the business is not easy. Prospective farmers might dream of earning a living from the earth, living in nature's beauty, and eating the freshest foods. But as Jesse Hirsch, staff writer for the *Modern Farmer* website, points out, "There's a big difference between ogling barn listings online and standing knee-deep in pig manure." If you think farming is all about stress-free sunsets and raising baby animals, you're "in for a rude awakening,"[6] according to Hirsch.

If you want to be a farmer and you were not born into a farm family, you should try living a farmer's life before committing to an agricultural career. This can be done by working as a farm apprentice for a season. Apprentices receive room and board and a small stipend while they absorb basic agriculture knowledge and skills. They learn to plant, harvest, weed, collect eggs, and feed animals.

Prospective apprentices can find organic farms to work on through an organization called World Wide Opportunities on Organic Farms (WWOOF). Members, called WWOOFers, are connected with farmers who provide room and board on sustainable farms in exchange for four to six hours of daily labor. The length of the visit can be tailored to last anywhere from one day to three or more months. WWOOF provides access to over twenty-one hundred organic farm hosts in the United States and thousands more in Africa, the Americas, the Asia-Pacific region, and Europe.

Starting a Farm

After working for a season or two as an apprentice, most people have enough experience to take a paying job on an established farm. Or they might be ready to commit to starting their own agricultural operation. This can be done in two ways: through leasing or buying land. Most experts recommend leasing, which is a cheaper option, though still expensive. In addition to paying a lease, beginning farmers need cash to purchase tools, seeds, animals, and other necessities.

Buying land has its own problems. In many desirable areas, agricultural land is being turned into suburban developments and strip malls. Even in farm states like Iowa, land prices have climbed more than 50 percent since 2010. Even if land seems affordable, most banks will not offer loans to new farmers because they are considered a business risk. However, since the government wants to encourage young farmers, the USDA offers loans of up to $300,000 through the Farm Service Agency. The program has an unusual caveat for a lender, though: A person must be turned down by three conventional banks before qualify for a government loan. Those who live in California have another option: A nonprofit organization called California FarmLink provides loans of up to $250,000 to underserved, low-income, beginning farmers across the state. FarmLink also maintains a database of land available for lease or sale.

Marketing Innovations

Most family farmers raise acres of corn and soybeans and keep a few dozen dairy cows, pigs, or chickens in the barn. Their earnings in any given year are dictated by commodity prices and government subsidies. But like nearly every other business, farming has changed in the twenty-first century, thanks to the Internet and social networking. A new generation of small farmers is involved with what is called community-supported agriculture (CSA). This might be described as alt-farming; farmers use the Internet, Facebook, and other social media sites to acquire a large network of consumers who pledge to financially support their farm operation. With CSAs, community "shareholders" put up money to cover a farmer's projected costs and salary. In return, the farmer shares the bounty of the land, delivering fresh—usually organic—meat, eggs, milk products, and fruits and veggies to the community throughout the growing season. Shareholders accept risks along with the farmers; they stand to lose their money if harvests are poor due to weather, insect infestations, or other problems. But by providing working capital, shareholders receive high-quality food for lower prices than they would pay at the grocery store. The farm becomes, in essence, the community's farm, with growers and consumers sharing the benefits and risks of producing food.

Using a tablet, a farmer records and monitors details on the health and productivity of his cows. Farmers may grow crops, raise livestock, or produce dairy products, but their daily work also requires knowledge of irrigation systems, seeds, chemicals, soil conditions, and more.

Some new farmers launch themselves into agriculture by signing up customers for a CSA and using the money to lease land and equipment. However, this can be a risky business; when hundreds of people put up thousands of dollars for delivered food, it better be good and plentiful if the farmer expects them to sign up for a second season.

Farmers can also add to their profits by providing entertainment in an agricultural setting, what some call agritainment. Farmers might host pick-your-own fruit events, Easter egg hunts for kids, or pumpkin patch costume parties around Halloween. Some plow mazes into their cornfields, while others operate farm museums, bed-and-breakfasts, or petting zoos. Nationally, more than fifty thousand farms in 2015 made at least a portion of their income from agritainment.

Filling a Farming Niche

"When we found our farm, my [fiancée] Kendra and I knew it was the right fit for us. It had plenty of run-down pasture for grazing animals, lots of semi-flat terrain for crops, a barn and corral that were in shambles, a defunct farmhouse that was livable, and—most importantly—lots of water. . . . We started our farm with a small, mixed garden plot; three pigs; two goats; and a handful of chickens. We . . . expanded our vegetable production area for the local farmers' markets . . . finding the niches in the market that we could fill, and figuring out what people would actually buy from our farm."

—Tyler Hoyt, owner of Green Table Farm

Tyler Hoyt, "We Want to Spend Our Lives Devoted to a Piece of Land," National Young Farmers Coalition, June 20, 2016. www.youngfarmers.org.

Job Outlook for Farmers

The Bureau of Labor Statistics (BLS) predicts that the number of agricultural workers will decline by 2 percent by 2024. This is due to economic factors; as prices increase on seeds, chemicals, land, and machinery, only well-funded farmers and large corporations will be able to afford farmland and pay to get crops into the ground. And the larger the farm, the better equipped it will be to withstand the unpredictable nature of the business, from bad weather to falling crop prices. However, the news isn't all bad for smaller farms. The BLS says that programs like the BFRDP will help a number of new farmers get into the agriculture business. Additionally, those with the business skills to develop CSAs, organic farms, and similar enterprises can expect to prosper as niche agriculture grows in popularity among city dwellers. There's little doubt that the world needs young farmers with innovative ideas, and if you understand the ups and downs of farming, you just might be watching the sunset over your well-tended field someday.

Find Out More

Beginning Farmer and Rancher Development Program (BFRDP)
website: https://nifa.usda.gov

This program was established by the US Department of Agriculture to encourage young people to become farmers. The BFRDP funds education and mentoring programs for new farmers.

National FFA Organization
PO Box 68960
6060 FFA Dr.
Indianapolis, IN 46268
website: www.ffa.org

Future Farmers of America (FFA) is the premier student organization for those interested in agriculture and related fields. The website provides information about FFA history and its mission, along with publications focused on agricultural education.

National Young Farmers Coalition (NYFC)
358 Warren St.
Hudson, NY 12534
website: www.youngfarmers.org

The NYFC is dedicated to helping young farmers who are willing to take a risk and work hard to support independent agriculture in the United States. The website features blogs, press media, and numerous resources related to farm training, jobs, resources, land leasing, and credit.

World Wide Opportunities on Organic Farms USA (WWOOF-USA)
654 Fillmore St.
San Francisco, CA 94117
website: www.wwoofusa.org

Program members can sign up to spend time on organic host farms, receiving room and board while learning about sustainable agriculture. WWOOFers under age eighteen need to be accompanied by a parent or guardian; children and pets are welcome for those over age eighteen.

Marine Biologist

A Few Facts

Median Salary
$62,610 in 2015

Minimum Educational Requirements
A bachelor's degree for most entry-level marine biology jobs; a PhD for those wishing to carry out independent research

Certification
Scuba certification necessary for some fieldwork

Personal Qualities
Love of science and marine life; good math, analytical, and communication skills; physically fit

Working Conditions
Outdoors in and near water; indoors in labs and offices

Number of Jobs
About 21,300 zoologists and wildlife biologists in 2014

Job Outlook
About 5 percent growth through 2022

If you have seen photos of the earth from outer space, then you know that roughly 70 percent of the earth's surface is covered by water. And yet scientists know more about the surface of the moon than they know about the oceans; if the seas were the size of this page, the area that has been fully explored would be the size of the period at the end of this sentence. That's why the world needs more marine biologists. These scientists study the oceans, the plants and animals that live in them, and how marine organisms interact with one another and the environment. Some marine biologists are even driven to study the ocean to find answers to "big questions" like where life began on earth and how humans evolved from creatures in the sea.

Marine biologists spend their workdays observing, protecting, and managing marine organisms from tiny microbes to kelp, coral, fish, and whales. The job might involve counting fish populations in a particular area, managing a marine wildlife preserve, or scuba diving to collect and catalog sponge species. Marine biologists work with diving equipment and boats and rely on cameras, notebooks, and computers to record their observations. Marine biologists also work in laboratories observing marine organisms, sequencing the organisms' DNA, and creating computer models to predict population growth or decline.

Marine biologists often specialize in a particular field. Some are environmental consultants for corporations, others work for the government as fish and wildlife biologists or fishery managers. Marine biologists called ichthyologists study the behavior, history, growth patterns, and environmental conditions of fish, usually focusing on one specific species. Oceanographers work in the biggest territory; they study the complex interactions that take place between the oceans, weather, currents, pollution, changing climate, sea life, and humanity. Whatever the exact job, marine biology is a great career for those who love to work outdoors and don't mind spending most of their workday soaking wet.

How Do You Become a Marine Biologist?

If you want to expand humanity's knowledge of the sea and its creatures and help solve pressing environmental problems along the way, marine biology might be a great career choice for you. Marine biologists are first and foremost biologists; high school students should take biology and chemistry courses along with math and physics. A good working knowledge of ecology and geography is also important for a prospective marine biologist. Good communication skills are also required. Marine biologists are primarily researchers; they take notes constantly, read and analyze scientific papers, and write intelligible articles, reports, and dissertations. Marine biology also involves writing concise grant proposals, understanding complex government regulations, presenting research findings at meetings and seminars, and drawing up budgets and schedules. Your high school writing classes should help you in this department.

However, marine biology is not all about course work and textbooks. If you live near the water, take scuba diving classes. While lessons can be expensive, there is definitely a payoff, as marine biologist Milton Love explains: "One of the quickest ways to get in good with researchers in college is to know how to dive. Researchers are always looking for cheap (read free) divers and, once you fulfill whatever requirements the college or university has for divers, you will likely find many happy offers for you to help out with someone's research."[7]

Love also recommends volunteering as a research assistant if you live near a college or university. He says biologists of any type—land or water—might take you on if your grades are good and you exhibit enthusiasm. And that experience will look great when you're applying to college.

Most institutions of higher learning in coastal states offer bachelor of science degrees in marine biology. Some of the most notable schools are the Scripps Research Institute, Woods Hole Oceanographic Institution, University of California–Santa Barbara, and the Rosenstiel School of Marine and Atmospheric Science at the University of Miami. Course work for a bachelor's degree in marine biology focuses on introductory biology, physics, inorganic and organic chemistry, calculus, oceanography, cell physiology, and ichthyology (the study of fish). If you wish to become an oceanographer, your courses will also include physics, math, and computer modeling. If you attend a school that is not near the ocean, you can pursue a degree in biology, fisheries, zoology, or other animal sciences.

Love writes that working toward a master's degree is important for prospective marine biologists: "You really should figure on going to graduate school if you want to go very far in the field."[8] Master's degree programs help students develop research and analytical skills and provide opportunities to participate in fieldwork studies. Those wishing to carry out independent research will need a PhD in marine biology, oceanography, fisheries, zoology, or related subjects like ecology or microbiology.

Where Do Marine Biologists Work?

A bachelor of science in marine biology is useful for those seeking work as technicians or assistants. People who hold a master's degree can work at a university and conduct experiments and fieldwork projects. Holders of PhDs can find employment with private companies, working as independent contractors to oversee short-term projects or solve specific problems. Zoos and aquariums often have research centers that employ marine biologists. Those who work as aquarium curators manage the entire collection of marine life found at places like the Birch Aquarium in San Diego, where three thousand fish live in more than sixty habitats.

Government agencies that study the geological, chemical, or physical aspects of marine environments hire the largest number of marine biologists. Those with advanced training, specialized skills, and strong research backgrounds can find employment with the National Oceanic and Atmospheric Administration (NOAA). NOAA oversees the National Ocean Service, the National Marine Fisheries Service, and other agencies that develop ecologically sound ways to use and protect ocean resources and improve our knowledge of sea environments. NOAA oceanographers also oversee aquaculture, or fish farming, and study the effects that fish farms have on the natural environment. Marine biologists at the US Environmental Protection Agency research the effects of pollution in waterways and the problems that toxic chemicals cause for sea life. The US Fish and Wildlife Service uses marine biologists to study and manage fish and endangered

Tagging and Tracking Sharks

"We've put over 200 [Global Positioning System] tags on white sharks . . . that ride on the animal and send us back the data. And what those satellite tags have taught us is when we tag a shark off the coast of Monterey Bay, it will travel thousands of miles—as far away as Hawaii—and halfway between Hawaii and California is an open region of the ocean that serves as a gathering spot of white sharks. And almost every white shark we tagged will go to this place. So our group dubbed it the White Shark Café."

—Barbara Block, marine biologist

Barbara Block, quoted in Ben Goldfarb, "A Leading Marine Biologist Works to Create a 'Wired Ocean,'" *Yale Environment 360*, March 20, 2013. http://e360.yale.edu.

marine life at national wildlife refuges, fish hatcheries, and national parks. Many states have similar agencies that retain the services of marine biologists.

One of the hottest new areas of specialization in private industry is in a field called marine biotechnology. People who work in this area are employed by pharmaceutical or energy companies. They spend their days creating new products based on the biodiversity of marine life. For example, biologists are studying ocean microbes to create new sources of biofuel, which can replace petroleum as a motor fuel. Drug companies are researching ways that ocean-based creatures, such as algae, sponges, and other aquatic life, can be used to create medicines for treating viral infections, cancer, inflammation, and other problems. Marine biotechnologists in this field are trained in bioinformatics, the practice of using computers, statistics, math, and engineering to analyze biological data. This information is being used to synthesize various experimental compounds in research laboratories.

Asking the Right Questions

"I think the biggest challenge [as a marine biologist] is to be able to ask the proper question so to arrive at the correct answer. After so many years of studying a single [fish] species, snook, [I] should have all of the answers. No such luck! After the correct question has been proffered, then how does one garner all the answers? Sometimes it is impossible for a single biologist to answer all the questions. It requires a team, and it becomes difficult to know who will find the proper solution and how the proper solution will be found."

—Ron Taylor, Florida program coordinator for snook

Ron Taylor, "Marine Fisheries Research: Ron Taylor," Florida Fish and Wildlife Conservation Commission, 2016. http://myfwc.com.

Environmental groups like the Ocean Conservancy hire marine biologists to conduct research to protect ocean habitats, monitor destructive fishing practices, and establish marine protected areas where sea life can thrive without human interference. Marine biologists in this role are often valued as ambassadors for the sea who can explain the geeky science to the general public. Marine biologist Richard Wylie says that communication is very important in this field. "The world's oceans are in a bad way with many, many years of pollution and overfishing," Wylie explains. "I feel that many of the issues that are [affecting] our marine environments could be addressed if more people were truly aware of what is actually going on . . . so we need to communicate the urgency of the problem to as many people as we possibly can."[9]

Marine biologist Barbara Block invented her own field of study. Block founded a program at Stanford University to place thousands of Global Positioning System tags on bluefin tuna, sharks, and twenty other species of large marine predators. These fish populations are under threat of collapse due to overfishing, and there is surprisingly little knowledge about the large, commercially valuable fish. Block is creating a "wired ocean" in which the trackers provide exact data as to where predator fish feed and spawn. The trackers are attached to the backs of fish at fish farms or in the ocean by divers. The chips send information about fish migration to satellites, which transfer the information to an app on a smartphone.

Working Indoors and Out

The public generally holds a romantic view of marine biologists, who are often seen in nature shows sailing across the wide open seas and scuba diving in stunning colonies of coral. In reality, most marine biologists spend five days indoors for every one working outdoors. They read articles in scientific journals, carry out lab work, analyze data to answer scientific questions, and draft and revise articles. The work often involves finding new solutions to tough problems, which requires patience, precision, and creativity in analyzing and interpreting data.

Like many other scientists, marine biologists rely on specialized high-tech equipment. They write their own computer code for conducting research and work with particle counters in the lab to tally microorganisms. Oxygen meters are used to measure respiration in marine organisms, while salinometers compute the salt levels in seawater. Marine biologists often pilot various types of research boats and compact submarines, which requires them to be experienced sailors. They must also be familiar with underwater cameras and robots, such as the remotely operated vehicles used to conduct research beneath the waves.

Conducting fieldwork in remote locations requires strength and stamina; the sea can be harsh and deadly. Living and working in a cramped boat on dangerous waters requires a strong commitment to the job. As Wylie explains, "When you're stuck out on the water getting soaked to the skin in the middle of a freezing winter night you need to be doing it for the love of it rather than the big bucks."[10]

Job Outlook

Marine biology is a highly competitive field. The work is mostly funded by government and private grants, meaning growth is limited by budgetary constraints. Wages for qualified marine biologists are expected to remain low, and the field is only expected to expand by 5 percent in the coming decade. However, factors, such as climate change, pollution, and population growth, will continue to impact marine environments. Whether conducting experiments in a lab, researching creatures underwater, or educating the public through environmental advocacy, the work of marine biologists will remain crucial for years to come.

Find Out More

American Fisheries Society (AFS)

425 Barlow Pl., Suite 110
Bethesda, MD 20814
website: http://fisheries.org

The eight thousand members of the AFS include fishery managers, biologists, ecologists, aquaculturists, and geneticists. The organization's website features blogs, profiles, articles about students and young professionals, job listings, career help, and other information.

Association of Zoos & Aquariums (AZA)

8403 Colesville Rd., Suite 710
Silver Spring, MD 20910
website: www.aza.org

The AZA focuses on animal conservation, science, recreation, and education as it relates to zoos and aquariums. The AZA website contains information about educational programs and materials pertaining to biology and animal display facilities.

MarineBio

1995 Fairlee Dr.
Encinitas, CA 92024
website: www.marinebio.org

MarineBio is a volunteer marine conservation and science education society working to provide the public with information about ocean life, marine biology, and marine conservation. The MarineBio website features a student section with education and career resources, information about marine biology degree programs, and frequently asked job interview questions.

Park Ranger

Most people think of park rangers as men and women who wear Smokey the Bear hats and spend their days giving nature talks, clearing brush from trails, and gazing out over the wilderness. And it's true, park rangers do all those things. But park rangers are also law enforcement officials who carry firearms, handcuffs, and other tools of the police trade. Rangers direct traffic, write tickets, bust vandals, and even tangle with outlaws and murderers. Most often rangers deal with hordes of unprepared tourists who visit parks by the millions each year. Nearly every park ranger has a story about rescuing someone who tried to take a selfie with a bear, tried to swim in an ice-cold raging river, or descended into the harsh environment of the Grand Canyon with little water or food.

Stewards, Teachers, Cops

Park rangers are sometimes called forest rangers. Their main mission is to act as stewards of America's public lands, preserving and protecting local, state, and national forests and parks. Rangers are educators; they give nature tours, design and create park exhibits, and give lectures to children and adults about natural, historical, and cultural aspects of a park. Some rangers conduct research, study wildlife, and monitor air and water quality in parks. A single workweek might consist of releasing rescued bear cubs into the wild, hosting a party of foreign dignitaries, and hunting feral pigs that are tearing up plants and harming native wildlife.

Park rangers also deal with government bureaucracy; they write reports, oversee budgets, and work with state and federal agencies to secure funding, implement environmental regulations, and regulate parks. When performing law enforcement duties, rangers patrol roads and trails on foot, on horseback, and in vehicles, such as ATVs, snowmobiles, and trucks. They are the first responders when accidents and natural disasters occur within a park. Those who work as rangers perform search-and-rescue missions for lost hikers and stranded mountain climbers. They provide first aid and emergency medical services and help recover bodies when accidents result in fatalities.

Andrea Lankford worked as a ranger for twelve years in national parks, including Zion in Utah, Yosemite in California, and the Grand Canyon in Arizona. She describes several aspects of her job:

> I directed traffic around tarantula jams. I pursued bad guys while galloping on horseback. I jumped into rescue helicopters bound for the depths of the Grand Canyon. I won arguments with bears. I dodged lightning bolts. I pissed on wildfires. I slept with rattlesnakes. I also saved endangered turtles, helped hikers get home, and saw a lifetime's worth of sunsets. It really was the best job in the world.[11]

Lankford also notes that her job was dangerous. National Park Service (NPS) rangers are more likely to be assaulted than any other federal officers, including drug enforcement agents. Nature can also take a toll on a park ranger's health. Rangers can get hit by lightning, drown, fall off a cliff, or fall victim to natural disasters, like wildfires and volcanic eruptions. Additionally,

Saving Endangered Species

"I loved . . . searching for sea turtle nests and documenting their locations [at North Carolina's Cape Hatteras National Seashore]. It felt like Christmas morning the day I discovered several turtles fighting their way up the sandy banks of their nest. The baby loggerheads were dark violet, like little bruises. . . . Holding [a] single turtle in my hands brought my decision about being a ranger into sharp focus. How could I not fight to keep this endangered species from becoming extinct? How could I not risk my life jumping from helicopters or fording rivers so that this baby turtle could someday return and lay its own eggs?"

—Andrea Lankford, retired national park ranger

Andrea Lankford, "Ranger Confidential: Secrets of National Park Rangers," *Backpacker*, September 2010. www.backpacker.com.

rangers are killed in plane and car crashes. Despite the dangers, there are plenty of positions for lovers of the outdoors who want a job that can be idyllic, dangerous, tedious, thrilling, and rewarding—all in a single day. A park ranger known as Rocky says of his job, "If the outdoors is your thing, there are few cooler ways to get paid while tromping around the forests, boating the lakes and rivers, and imparting your outdoor knowledge to children and adults alike."[12]

Where Do Rangers Work?

When most people envision rangers in their crisp uniforms and iconic hats, they are thinking of park rangers who work for the NPS. The NPS operates 412 sites, including national parks, monuments, battlefields, historical parks, lakeshores, seashores, and scenic rivers and trails. The park service works to protect these places in a pristine natural state, what the NPS describes as unimpaired for future generations.

Park rangers also work for the US Forest Service (USFS), which manages 154 national forests and 20 grasslands. Rangers who work for the USFS are commonly known as forest rangers or district rangers (they oversee a segment of a national forest called a district).

While many people confuse the USFS with the NPS, the federal agencies have different goals. The forest service promotes the concept of "multiple use," which means the USFS accommodates both nature lovers and commercial enterprises. Forest rangers deal with hikers, campers, boaters, hunters, and fishers who visit national forests for recreational purposes. USFS rangers also regulate businesses involved in grazing, logging, mining, drilling, and other endeavors that are not permitted in national parks.

America's sprawling national forests are much larger than national parks and much less regulated. While illegal activities take place in national parks, crimes occur much more often in national forests. Rangers have to deal with illegal dumping, non-permitted hunting and fishing, and theft of wood and other natural resources. In some national forests, rangers face off with drug gangs that grow marijuana in isolated areas and pollute the land with toxic pesticides and other chemicals. In such cases rangers conduct raids with other law enforcement officials and later return to the sites to remove irrigation pipes, camping gear, and trash. In California a ranger might participate in four to eight marijuana eradication raids a year.

In addition to enforcing the law, a USFS ranger's workday might include approving permits for mining or logging operations, maintaining trails and outbuildings, and conducting controlled burns to remove underbrush from mature forests. Like park rangers, forest rangers patrol campgrounds, give nature lectures to the public, conduct search-and-rescue operations, and provide emergency first aid when required.

The federal government also employs rangers at the Bureau of Land Management, which manages over 245 million acres (99 million ha) of public lands that are not generally tourist destinations. These rangers investigate crimes, such as natural resource theft, hazardous material dumping, arson, and vandalism at archaeological sites. Rangers also work for the Fish and Wildlife Service (FWS), which manages the National Wildlife Refuge System—562 wildlife refuges spread throughout the fifty states set aside to conserve fish, wildlife, and plants. Rangers employed by the FWS engage in biological monitoring, habitat conservation, heavy equipment operation, fire management, law enforcement, visitor services, and environmental education. Not all rangers work for the federal government; state and local governments also oversee parks, public lands, and wildlife areas, where rangers might find employment.

How to Become a Park Ranger

Some professionals go to school to become ecologists, anthropologists, sociologists, or historians. Others take classes in museum science, police science, business administration, or natural resource management. Those who wish to become a park ranger need to understand all of these subjects and more. Any high school student hoping to become a park ranger should learn about the municipal, state, and national park systems and take courses that focus on conservation, ecology, forestry, botany, biology, earth science, forensics, and anthropology. In college aspiring park rangers pursue relevant majors, such as environmental sciences, park and recreation management, wildlife and forestry, horticulture, police science, natural resource management, fisheries and wildlife law enforcement, and biological sciences.

Prospective park rangers who wish to apply to the NPS or the USFS are required to meet what the federal government calls a GS-5 qualification. Those at a GS-5 level have a bachelor's degree in any subject. That said, the NPS seeks applicants with at least twenty-four credit hours in one or more related subjects, including natural resource management, earth sciences, archaeology, museum sciences, behavioral science, and public administration. (A complete list can be found on the NPS website.) Most municipal and state ranger jobs have similar requirements. Anyone interested in seeking positions at local or state levels should inquire at the specific agency that oversees the park and wildlife management systems.

Ranger positions also require law enforcement training, which means applicants need a clean record. Rangers undergo a thorough and intense background check. While an applicant's traffic tickets and minor misdemeanors might be overlooked, those with citations for driving while intoxicated or long rap sheets can forget their dreams of becoming a park ranger. Background investigation can take months, and prospective candidates must also pass regular drug tests.

Internships and Volunteer Organizations

Many park rangers say they took the first steps on their career path in high school when they volunteered for part-time summer jobs at local parks. Seasonal volunteers run concession stands, clean bathrooms, maintain trails and buildings, and help with programs, demonstrations, and tours related to nature and local history. Sometimes these jobs pay a small salary.

Another way to lay the foundation for a park ranger career is to join a "friends of the park" group at a local or state park. These groups sponsor nature walks, conduct cleanups, publicize park programs, and engage in other hands-on activities. Ranger Rocky explains the benefits of such programs: "These groups are large, organized, and actually have some sway with how the park is managed simply because of the sheer amount of grunt work and fundraising they do to better the place. Joining such a group will not only get you [noticed] but it is also an amazing way to get to know the ins and outs of that particular park."[13]

On a federal level, the NPS offers high school, college, and graduate students numerous volunteer and internship opportunities in national parks. Most positions are offered at a local level; those who are interested can contact the specific park where they wish to volunteer. Future park rangers can also participate in numerous organizations to gain experience. The Youth Conservation Corps, affiliated with the NPS, offers summer employment to high school students ages fifteen through eighteen. Members work at national park sites, where they learn about ecology, conservation, and preservation of public lands. The Student Conservation Association places around twenty-six hundred high school and young adult volunteers annually at jobs in parks, public lands, and urban green spaces.

The Bad with the Good

Journalist Nathan Rott writes that there's an old saying among NPS employees: "We get paid in sunrises and sunsets."[14] This is a reminder that the pay for park rangers is not great. The work is seasonal, the hours are long, and rangers can be transferred from one place to another with little prior notice. The job involves a lot of manual labor, outdoors in heat, cold, rain, and snow. Rangers work weekends and holidays because those are the most popular times for visitors. The job can be hard on families; rangers might be stationed hundreds of miles from their homes, spouses, and children. However, as rangers spend more time on the job, they can eventually be assigned a permanent position at a park. Those with the most education and experience can earn a better salary as managers supervising other park employees. Those with the longest time on the job can become park superintendents.

While park rangers can only expect to earn little more than $35,000 annually, those who work for the government receive benefits, such as health care and pension plans. Rangers are also provided with free housing and most of the gear they need to perform their jobs, including uniforms and tools. And those sunrises and sunsets provide benefits that cannot be measured in monetary terms. "Park rangers are used to getting told, 'You've got the best job in the world,'" says park ranger Stacy Czebotar. "And we agree with people who say that—because we know it's true."[15]

Find Out More

National Park Service (NPS)
5200 Glover Rd. NW
Washington, DC 20015
website: www.nps.gov

The NPS oversees all 412 national parks in the United States and its territories and provides detailed information about each one on its website. Job seekers can learn about the NPS application process, and students can find out about internships and volunteer opportunities.

ParkRangerEdu.org
website: www.parkrangeredu.org

This independent educational resource exists to inform students and others seeking careers as state or federal park rangers. The website explores many aspects of the job, including environmental sustainability, law enforcement, training, education, state-to-state job requirements, and salaries.

Student Conservation Association (SCA)
4245 N. Fairfax Dr., Suite 825
Arlington, VA 22203
website: www.thesca.org

The aim of the SCA is to build the next generation of conservation leaders. The organization's membership includes people from all fifty states interested in green careers, age fifteen to young adult, including high school and college students and recent graduates. Members work to protect, improve, and restore national parks, marine sanctuaries, cultural landmarks, and urban green spaces across the United States.

Wildland Firefighter

Dramatic images of wildland firefighters facing off against towering infernos in western forests are a staple of American news shows and websites on most days between May and November. In 2016 Agriculture Secretary Tom Vilsack told *USA Today* that extremely destructive wildfires are the new normal. Vilsack pointed out that the wildfire season is now seventy-eight days longer (on average) than it was in 1970, and there has been a sevenfold increase in the number of fires burning more than 10,000 acres (4,047 ha) in the West. By the end of August 2016, the new normal could be seen in Southern California, where thousands of firefighters slogged through the heat, smoke, and difficult terrain to fight wildland fires that burned at more than 1,500°F (816°C).

The motto of the wildland firefighter is to protect lives, houses, and property—in that order. Many people consider firefighters to be heroes, and for good reason—they have one of the toughest jobs imaginable. The US Forest Service (USFS) describes the job realistically: "If you like hiking without trails; packing between 40 and 120 pounds of food, water, and supplies on your back; eating and sleeping in the dirt for days on end; and not having consistent showers, then you may be interested in becoming a wildland firefighter."[16]

Regulations say a wildland firefighter can be asked to work sixteen-hour days fourteen days in a row before receiving two days off. However, when fires are very bad, firefighters can be made to work an extra seven days. Wildland firefighter Drew Miller describes how this schedule works: "You might spend most of a month constantly firefighting, then get a mere two days to recuperate. When somebody asks how your month has been, you can honestly answer 'on fire.'"[17]

Fighting wildfires is dirty, dangerous work, and firefighters face lethal hazards. Wildfires often break out when it is very windy and hot—between 85°F and 110°F (29°C and 43°C)—and fighting fires under these conditions can be life-threatening. Firefighters face dehydration, heatstroke, and heart attacks. Fires also produce smoke, dust, and extremely hazardous gases, including carbon monoxide, sulfur dioxide, and formaldehyde. Little wonder that one of the main hazards of the job is what firefighters call eating smoke. Additionally, firefighters are killed in vehicle accidents, by falling tree limbs known as widow makers, by collapsing buildings, and even by drowning in the deluge of water dropped from firefighting tanker aircraft.

For a wildland firefighter, survival depends on having above-average physical strength and stamina. Firefighters also need the ability to stay calm in emergencies and make critical decisions as quickly as a fire can change direction. Firefighters often interact with extremely stressed-out and frightened citizens who are leaving their homes during an evacuation. This requires excellent communication skills, which are also necessary when dealing with government officials and the media. And wildland firefighters are not in it for the money; they are driven to serve the public out of a sense of honor and duty.

How Fires Are Fought

The elite wildland firefighters who work in the toughest conditions are called hotshots. When a fire begins, hotshots set up a command center at an anchor point near the safest, or coldest, edge of the fire. This is meant to ensure there is a barrier between the firefighters and burning vegetation. Crews then construct fire lines, or firebreaks, from anchor points. Fire lines are the main weapon used to put out wildfires; fires need three things to burn—heat, oxygen, and fuel. The only way to stop a wildfire is to deprive it of fuel, which means hotshot teams clear trees, shrubs, and other vegetation down to the bare dirt, or what they refer to as the "mineral soil." After all flammable fuel on a fire line is removed from the path of a fire, the flames go out. In heavily forested areas fire lines can be more than 100 feet (30 m) wide. However, if it is windy a fire can jump a fire line, forcing crews to regroup at a new spot to cut new fire lines. Air tankers, which can drop up to 3,000 gallons (11,356 L) of water or fire retardant, are used to help crews maintain fire lines.

Eventually, enough fire lines are in place to contain a wildfire. At this time, firefighters search for hotspots near the fire lines that need to be extinguished with water and flame retardant chemicals, such as ammonium phosphate. Firefighters who do this work refer to themselves as ground pounders; they spread water on smoldering trees and brush. When water is not available, burning material and coals are covered with dirt. This work often requires firefighters to work all night—slogging through two twelve-hour shifts in a row.

When wildfires start in remote areas, firefighters called smoke jumpers are called in. Smoke jumpers parachute from airplanes and work to extinguish small fires immediately, before they become major disasters. Helitack crews are firefighters who are specially trained to rappel down ropes from hovering helicopters. Their primary job is to leave fire-suppression equipment and supplies on the ground for ground pounders. Firefighting helicopters and airplanes that dump flame retardant are operated by specially trained commercial pilots who are not necessarily firefighters.

Other specialized groups of wildland firefighters include fire engine crews that operate heavy off-road vehicles that carry up to 800 gallons (3,028 L) of water or foam fire retardant. Other positions include sawyers, specialists who cut down trees, and lookouts who ensure crew safety by watching for approaching flames. There are about five hundred of these hand crews in the United States, each with twenty firefighters who are trained to put out fires. Whatever a wildland firefighter's exact job, safety is the number one concern. Crews create large safe zones in clearings or previously burned areas where they can retreat if threatened by flames.

Clothing and Tools

Wildland firefighters cut fire lines with chain saws and shovels. A wood-handled tool called a Pulaski (invented by USFS employee Ed Pulaski in 1910) has an ax blade on one side and a small pickax called a cutter mattock on the other side. Firefighters use this tool to cut through matted brush and to clear loose surface materials. Firefighters also carry a McLeod, a combination heavy-duty rake and hoe tool named after the inventor, ranger Malcolm McLeod. Fire line–cutting bulldozers are another important tool that must be manned by firefighters.

Firefighters wear heavy protective gear and carry safety devices. Their clothing includes fire-resistant pants, shirts, and gloves; heavy leather boots; a fire helmet; and eye protection. Gas masks help alleviate problems associated with smoke inhalation, which can cause coughing, nausea, and even death. A device called a fire shelter is little bigger than a sleeping bag and is used as a last resort when a firefighter is trapped near flames and cannot escape. The shelter is made with layers of aluminum foil, silica, and fiberglass and is meant to reflect heat and trap breathable air inside.

How to Become a Wildland Firefighter

Wildland firefighters are generally employed by federal or state government agencies. On the federal level, hotshots work for the National Park Service, the USFS, the Bureau of Land Management, and the US Fish and Wildlife Service. Similar wildlife and land management agencies are found at the state level, and they work with local fire and rescue departments. Anyone who wishes to work for the federal government must be a US citizen and at least eighteen years of age. Anyone wishing to work at the state level should check the state's government website for further information. Many wildfire fighting agencies offer internships and volunteer positions. To qualify, candidates must be at least eighteen and meet various medical, physical, and certification standards. Interns and volunteers usually perform the full range of duties of a professional firefighter, and the experience improves their chances of finding a full-time job as a wildland firefighter.

Before a person can become a wildland firefighter, he or she must be sponsored by a local fire department or a state or federal agency affiliated with the National Wildfire Coordinating Group (NWCG). The NWCG develops guidelines, qualifications, and training standards for firefighters.

Federal and state agencies require wildland firefighters to have a certificate called an Incident Qualification Card, commonly called a Red Card. This card is accepted by most wildland firefighting agencies and proves that the holder has the training and physical abilities necessary to work as a firefighter. A Red Card can be obtained by taking two basic wildland fire training courses

A wildland firefighter sprays water on flames in an effort to prevent the spread of fire to populated areas at the edge of a forest. These firefighters must be able to work long hours in hot, dangerous conditions and carry their supplies on their backs while hiking through rough terrain.

referred to as S-130 Firefighter Training and S-190 Introduction to Wildland Fire Behavior. (These separate courses, available through the NWCG, are usually taken together and referred to as S-130/S-190 for short.)

The S-130 training provides introductory skills needed by all wildland firefighters. Twelve courses, lasting one to three hours, are based on a system called LCES, which stands for lookouts, communications, escape routes, and safety zones. Online courses cover topics such as constructing and reinforcing fire lines, extinguishing fires, fire investigation, and using fire shelters, pumps, and fire engines. The course wraps up with a hands-on Field Day Exercise in which firefighters demonstrate their skills with hand tools, drip torches, fire shelters, pumping equipment, and other firefighting devices. As the title makes clear, the S-190 Introduction to Wildland Fire Behavior course provides information about the ways wildfires behave. The online courses cover the charac-

Saving Lives, Not Houses

"Houses are deathtraps in a fire. That's why . . . the proper procedure is to pretty much ignore them. We let houses burn down. We understand how important they are to people, and we'll try to stop them from catching fire in the first place, but once they go up, we're not going to risk our lives to save them. We don't even know how—we're not structural firefighters. . . . It's a different story if there are occupants inside but if it comes down to saving your house and letting the fire advance or losing it and controlling the burn, we always choose the latter."

—Drew Miller, wildland firefighter

Drew Miller, "5 Ways Wildfire Fighting Is Exactly as Insane as It Sounds," Cracked, March 25, 2014. www.cracked.com.

teristics of a wildfire environment and how interactions between heat, wind, and fuel influence a fire's behavior.

Wildland firefighters must pass online tests given by the NWCG, correctly answering at least 70 percent of the questions associated with S-130/S-190 courses. And firefighters must also take a tough physical test before receiving Red Cards. The Work Capacity Test is used to qualify individuals for the three levels of wildland firefighting duty: arduous, moderate, and light. While the moderate and light tests are given to those with less rigorous jobs, such as safety officers and fire behavior analysts, wildland firefighters must pass the Arduous Pack Test. This requires a firefighter to carry a 45-pound (20-kg) pack and complete a 3-mile (4.8-km) hike in forty-five minutes. That means fast-walking at 4 miles per hour (6.4 kph) up and down hills while carrying a heavy pack.

While the NWCG is the main source for S-130/S-190 courses and tests, a few colleges offer the programs to those studying fire science or forestry. And prospective firefighters can increase their chances of finding work if they earn a degree in fire science. Students seeking such degrees often work on a firefighting crew for a semester.

Getting a Job

Anyone hoping to work at a federal agency must be an American citizen who speaks English. Because of the physical demands of the job, wildland firefighters must be between the ages of eighteen and thirty-five when they are hired.

Despite the dangers and hardships associated with the job, the employment field for wildland firefighters is very competitive. About ten thousand people work as wildland firefighters. Most are part-time firefighters, called seasonals, who sign on for a limited number of hours during the fire season. Seasonals often work as park rangers or foresters when not fighting fires. Seasonals in the Northwest work from mid-June to October. In California the fire season starts in early May. In the Southeast seasonal firefighters start in the early fall. Firefighting agencies also hire permanent seasonal firefighters, who work twenty-six weeks on and twenty-six weeks off. There are also several thousand full-time wildland firefighters working for government agencies. They normally work forty-hour workweeks; when not battling flames, they conduct prescribed burns and thin underbrush to lessen the risk of wildfires. Permanent seasonal and full-time firefighters receive good government benefits, such as retirement, health and life insurance, paid vacation, and sick leave.

Find Out More

Fire and Aviation Management
3833 S. Development Ave.
Boise, ID 83705
website: www.nps.gov/fire/wildland-fire/about.cfm

This branch of the National Park Service is dedicated to aggressively putting out unwanted fires in national parks. The website features stories from experienced firefighters and information about wildland firefighter training, jobs, and apprenticeships.

National Wildfire Coordinating Group (NWCG)

website: www.nwcg.gov

This federal agency develops guidelines, qualifications, and training standards for firefighters working for numerous agencies, including the National Park Service, the US Forest Service, and the US Fish and Wildlife Service. The NWCG website provides online training courses, job aids, and other information about how to become a wildfire fighter.

National Wildfire Suppression Association (NWSA)

PO Box 330

Lyons, OR 97358

website: http://nwsa.publishpath.com

The NWSA represents private wildfire service contractors, with a website that contains job listings and information about firefighter training programs and obtaining an Incident Qualification Card.

Horticulturist

A Few Facts

Median Salary
$40,850 in 2015

Minimum Educational Requirements
Bachelor of science degree in horticulture, botany, or related fields

Personal Qualities
Knowledge of plants and cultivation, statistical analysis skills, organized, enjoys teamwork, not afraid to get hands dirty

Working Conditions
Outdoors in gardens in all kinds of weather; indoors in greenhouses and labs

Number of Jobs
Approximately 300,000 in 2015

Job Outlook
A 2 percent decline by 2022

Most people who love the outdoors love plants. But horticulturists *really* love plants. They specialize in horticulture: the science, art, and industry of plant cultivation in gardens, orchards, and nurseries. Horticulturists love planting plants, pruning, weeding, watering, and digging in the dirt. They work with plants that bear fruits, berries, nuts, herbs, vegetables, and flowers. When horticulturists aren't physically working with plants, they are researching plants, designing gardens, or studying better growing methods.

Horticulturists work in rural farm fields and in large greenhouses. Some are urban growers who beautify city parks and arboretums with ornamental flowers, trees, and shrubs. Horticulturists with a focus on improving the environment specialize in low-water gardens, native plants, and organic fertilizers and pest management. Horticulturists in urban areas are making cities more livable by expanding green spaces where the natural environment bumps up against concrete and asphalt. Urban horticulturists specialize in rooftop gardens, small pocket parks, and rain gardens that use runoff from sidewalks and parking lots. Other ecological tasks associated with horticulture include using plants to reduce erosion and stabilize slopes, improve air and water quality, and provide a buffer of shade around buildings to keep them cool.

Horticulturists may also find employment maintaining golf courses or turf on sports fields. Horticultural researchers work with seed companies and food producers to breed new plant varieties and increase yields. Some breed drought- or pest-resistant plants for vegetable farms, vineyards, orchards, and olive groves. Horticulturists work for government agencies, including local park departments, county or state agricultural agencies, and federal agencies, such as the US Department of Agriculture (USDA) and the National Park Service. Horticulturists can also be self-employed; they grow and sell fruits and vegetables, work as landscapers, own garden centers, or provide vegetation for special events like weddings.

An emerging field called therapeutic horticulture focuses on creating natural environments to help people cope with mental or physical illnesses. Horticultural therapists design, plant, and maintain gardens at hospitals, health care institutions, retirement centers, treatment centers, and even prisons. Therapeutic gardens are easily accessible, with raised plant beds that can be enjoyed by those with limited physical movement. The gardens are designed to highlight the healing elements of nature, with fountains, waterfalls, and plants that stimulate the senses with notable colors, fragrances, and textures. A horticultural therapist might also work as an instructor who teaches gardening, an activity known to alleviate depression, improve motor skills, and encourage communication and problem solving.

How to Become a Horticulturist

Prospective horticulturists can take the first steps on their career path in high school by focusing on biology, ecology, and earth sciences. A bachelor of science degree in horticulture, botany, or a related field is required for most jobs in horticulture production,

A Rewarding Occupation

"There are so many things I enjoy about my job. I enjoy the blend of science and art. I love working outside and being surrounded by such beauty each day. I love that there will always be something new to learn; new plants, new gardening techniques, etc. The experience of seeing plants develop over time—throughout the year and from one year to another—is pretty amazing. And I get to work with creative, passionate, and friendly people who are willing to work hard for not-great wages because they believe in this labor of love. This is a highly rewarding job."

—Crystal, horticulturist

Crystal, "Career Day: Horticulturist," Aspiring Mormon Women, January 24, 2014. http://aspiringmormonwomen.org.

management, and marketing. College courses focus on soil science, chemistry, botany, and forestry, with lab work in plant cultivation and breeding. Some schools also offer a bachelor of arts in horticulture, with a focus on planning events, designing gardens, and creating educational programs, such as school gardens. Students with an interest in horticultural therapy can take courses that emphasize the therapeutic aspects of botany and landscape design.

A master of science degree in horticulture is important for those who wish to work in horticultural research and education. Master's programs focus on plant genetics, breeding, propagation, and the production, handling, and marketing of ornamental plants. Biotechnology is a fast-growing segment of the economy, and horticulturists with advanced degrees are in demand in the biotech industry. Biotech horticulturists are working to produce new varieties of plants for use as food and drugs. Biotech courses include molecular biology, genetics, biochemistry, and cell biology.

Internships, Scholarships, and Volunteer Opportunities

Since horticulture often involves hands-on physical work, students can gain valuable experience by enrolling in internships and volunteer programs that allow them to work in the field and advance their skills. Programs are available at a wide range of institutions, including botanical gardens, arboretums, and horticultural societies. Interns and volunteers learn basic gardening techniques and become familiar with tools, equipment, and landscaping machinery. They learn how horticultural institutions operate and develop teamwork skills. A horticulturalist named Crystal describes her intern experiences at the Smithsonian Gardens in Washington, DC, and the Royal Botanic Gardens in London:

> I did two internships on my own after graduation, to gain practical experience and get a feel for public gardening. . . . Not only did I gain good practical skills and more plant knowledge from both experiences, but I also found out that a public garden was where I wanted to be. I loved the idea of creating and maintaining beautiful garden spaces that would provide learning opportunities for others.[18]

While they help flowers grow, students can shrink their college debt with horticulture scholarships. The USDA offers two scholarship programs. The USDA/1890 National Scholars Program is open to those pursuing a bachelor's degree in agriculture, horticulture, and related fields at one of the institutions known as the 1890 Historically Black Land-Grant Universities, which include Alabama A&M University, Central State University in Ohio, Fort Valley State University in Georgia, Kentucky State University, and fourteen others. The goal of the scholarship program is to increase the number of students of color in horticulture and other natural resource sciences. Scholarships provide full tuition, room and board, and employment opportunities. Horticulture students can also participate in the USDA's Public Service Leaders

Scholarship Program, which provides paid internships that can become permanent jobs upon graduation.

Horticulture grants and scholarships are also provided by the Garden Club of America, the Anne S. Chatham Fellowship in Medicinal Botany, and the Douglas Dockery Fellowship in Garden History and Design. Numerous colleges and universities also offer scholarships, including the University of California–Davis and the University of Wisconsin–Madison.

To improve chances of success, applicants should first seek volunteer positions at arboretums, botanical gardens, or nature preserves. A good way to show initiative is to organize a shoreline cleanup along a beach, lake, or river, or a community restoration of a neglected public park or garden.

Horticulture at a World-Class Botanical Garden

There are a wide variety of jobs available to horticulturists, and many of them can be found at the San Diego Zoo Safari Park in Escondido, California. The 1,800-acre (728-ha) Safari Park is home to 3,500 wild and endangered animals representing 260 species. The park also features a world-class botanical garden with more than 1.7 million plants. The San Diego Zoo Safari Park department employs thirty-five horticulturists. Some focus on maintaining a specific area of a hundred or so acres, while others specialize in African or Asian plants, forestry, irrigation, or pest control.

One of the biggest challenges to the zoo's horticulturists comes from the demand to re-create exotic native habitats for the zoo's animals. For example, the zoo features African animals, such as giraffes, elephants, and tigers, but many African plants will not grow in California's climate, which is relatively drier and cooler than the African savanna. This means horticulturists are tasked with propagating African plants that tolerate drought and cold. The park foliage must also be protected from native animals, such as rabbits, deer, and squirrels that eat the plants, dig them up, or use them for nesting materials.

A Relationship with Nature

"Working with plants requires a lot of optimism, but at its best is a real and pure pursuit. It requires the husbandry of earth and cooperation with elements that we may normally protect ourselves from, and there's a great reward that comes with pulling harvest after a hard but fulfilling relationship. [Horticulture] is one of the great experiments, and forces us to be interested and curious or find eventual failure."

—Ezra Gardiner, horticulturist

Ezra Gardiner, quoted in Amanda Sullivan, "Interview with a Plant Whisperer," *Old Edwards Inn & Spa* (blog), February 4, 2016. http://blog.oldedwardsinn.com.

While some work to protect plants, horticulturists in the zoo's Browse Department specialize in growing food to feed the exotic animals. Every year, horticulturists at the San Diego Zoo Safari Park produce 20 tons (18 metric tons) of acacia to feed giraffes and gorillas. Around two hundred thousand pieces of eucalyptus from thirty-four different species are grown to feed koalas (some is shipped to other zoos where koalas live throughout the United States). The park's horticulturists grow 15 tons (13.6 metric tons) of bamboo for giant pandas and red pandas. And 60 tons (54.4 metric tons) of fig foliage is produced for the zoo's elephants, tapirs, bonobos, and forest buffalo.

Some of the zoo's horticulturists work for San Diego Zoo Global, a project dedicated to conserving and propagating endangered plants. The plants come from nearly everywhere, from the nearby Santa Catalina Island off the Southern California coast to distant Australia and Algeria. Since the plants are endangered in their native habitat, the zoo's horticulturists help increase their numbers by propagating them in the park and preserving their seeds in the San Diego Zoo Global Seed Bank. Horticulturists working for the San Diego Zoo Institute for Conservation Research work to restore native vegetation and highlight the San Diego region's biodiversity. When they are not working at the zoo, the horticulturists attend botanical conferences, help replant native plants in local areas scorched by wildfires, and study trees in rain forests from the Amazon to Africa.

You Need to Be Fit and Efficient

Horticulture is hard work. People in the profession often lift and move heavy plants and soil; wield rakes, shovels, and other garden tools; and work outdoors in all sorts of conditions. To be a horticulturist, you must love getting your hands dirty. Elise Newman, who blogs for the San Diego Zoo Global *ZooNooz*, sums up the work of the horticulturists at the San Diego Zoo Safari Park: "These horticulturists are fit, efficient women and men who face risks every day. In addition to working outdoors in 100+ degree Fahrenheit temperatures, they operate heavy machinery including chain saws, wood chippers, and dump trucks. They avoid rattlesnakes, thorns, bugs, sunburn, dehydration, and rainstorms. And they do it all with (amazingly) positive attitudes."[19]

Not all horticulturists spend their time digging in the dirt. Garden designers often work indoors on computers using design software apps, including Realtime Landscaping and Home Designer Suite. Some work in greenhouses, while those in the biotech industry spend their days in labs peering into microscopes. And it helps to be free of allergy or asthma problems; horticulturists are exposed to plant pollen and other allergens and often handle chemical pesticides, fertilizers, and herbicides.

Job Outlook and Salaries

The number of horticultural jobs is basically static; the field is expected to shrink slightly by 2022. And while a career in horticulture has many rewards, few of them are financial. Those with a bachelor's degree who begin their careers in botanical gardens, greenhouses, landscape design firms, or garden centers can expect to make a little over $30,000 a year. However, horticulturists with several years of experience can earn between $40,000 and $75,000 annually, depending on the job, the company, and the level of responsibility. For example, horticulturists who work as managers supervising crop production earn about $61,200. The salary for horticulturists who work in agricultural research and development is $62,210 for those who specialize in food science; the study of the physical, biological, and chemical makeup of food. Soil and plant specialists, who develop ways to increase yields and improve crop quality, can earn $69,470. Nursery and greenhouse managers with bachelor's degrees brought in a median annual wage of $64,460 in 2013.

The career news is good for those in the field of horticultural therapy. The number of jobs for all occupational therapists is expected to expand by 30 percent by 2022, and horticultural therapy is expected to experience similar growth. While the Bureau of Labor Statistics does not keep separate salary statistics for horticultural therapists, occupational therapists earned a median income of $76,940 in 2013.

Find Out More

AmericanHort
525 Ninth St. NW, Suite 800
Washington, DC 20004
website: https://americanhort.org

AmericanHort includes greenhouse and nursery growers, plant retailers and distributors, interior and exterior landscapers, florists, students, educators, and others. The group's website features material about awards programs, horticultural research, the HortScholars program for students, and career info.

American Horticultural Therapy Association
610 Freedom Business Center, #110
King of Prussia, PA 19406
website: http://ahta.org

This organization promotes the use of horticulture as a method of healing those with physical and mental illnesses. Its website contains details about the work, educational opportunities, internships, and job listings.

US Department of Agriculture (USDA)

1400 Independence Ave. SW
Washington, DC 20250
website: www.usda.gov

The USDA oversees food, agriculture, natural resources, rural development, nutrition, and related issues for the federal government. The agency's website provides links to government horticulture programs, the USDA/1890 National Scholars Program, and the Public Service Leaders Scholarship Program.

Adventure Tour Guide

A Few Facts

Median Salary
$41,000 in 2015

Minimum Educational Requirements
None, but a certification in wilderness first aid is helpful when seeking employment

Personal Qualities
Group leader, hard worker, physically fit, public speaker, cooking skills, patience

Working Conditions
Outdoors in all types of weather, oftentimes in harsh and dangerous conditions; seasonal work, no regular hours

Number of Jobs
Approximately 10,000 in 2016

Job Outlook
About 5 percent growth by 2025

Of all the careers available to those who love the outdoors, perhaps nothing spells excitement more than working as an adventure tour guide. After all, the word *adventure* is in the job title. Adventure tour guides work in the United States and on nearly every continent conducting tours in some of the most visually stunning places on earth. They might lead a group of sightseers through a pristine mountain pass on horseback or bounce them over churning rapids in a whitewater raft. Some tour guides take inexperienced tourists down hiking trails; others provide leadership for experienced hunters, fishers, and mountain climbers. And while it is true that adventure tour guides experience many exciting escapades on the job, they also have great responsibilities; at all times they need to know where they are, what they are doing, and what dangers may lie ahead.

Job one for an adventure tour guide is to provide a safe, positive outdoor experience for those they lead. Tour guides also need skills in cooking, customer service, and public speaking. The hard work part is obvious; tour guides are expected to hike, bike, backpack, raft, ski, or kayak twenty-plus days a month during the busy seasons. They also have to prepare all gear and food before a trip, help guests with their packs and tents, repair gear in the field, and lead camp cleanups. Guides are often expected to provide full meals for their clients, although some have assistants to help cook and serve.

While sweating it out in the sun and freezing in the cold, adventure tour guides are expected to provide service with a smile—working well with customers is one of the most important aspects of the job. People on tours pay good money for their adventures and are often inexperienced. Guides must love working with people and do everything in their power to remain positive and respectful in sometimes trying circumstances. Guides usually contact their guests two weeks before a tour, conduct orientation sessions before a trip, and provide guests with the basic knowledge they will need to have a memorable experience.

As group leaders, guides are expected to be fun, funny, and engaging while expertly describing the history, geology, and flora and fauna of the area they are exploring. And as outdoor tour guide Julie Trevelyan states, when someone asks her the name of a bird or lizard that she doesn't know, "I might make something up on the fly." According to Trevelyan, "telling tall tales & making stuff up is sometimes a job requirement when guiding. So that's why I'll call [a bird I can't identify] a Cretaceous Blue-Rimmed Phalanges layer/Red-tailed Hawk. . . . Because you're going to believe me no matter what."[20] Trevelyan does point out that she sometimes gets busted by an expert in birds or botany. In such cases she learns as much as she can from that person.

Wilderness Therapy

Wilderness experiences are considered good therapy for any stressed-out urbanite. But the field of wilderness therapy, which has emerged in the past few decades, does not focus on providing calming experiences for city-bred hipsters. Instead, wilderness therapy guides work with young adults and others struggling with addiction and behavioral or psychological issues. The idea behind wilderness therapy is that when young people spend time alone in nature, they reflect on their lives and develop more realistic and positive perceptions of themselves.

Wilderness therapists follow a variety of programs. Some programs are simply centered on hiking, camping, and canoeing, while others involve tough tasks, such as rock climbing or river rafting. The challenges are meant to build self-reliance and self-respect and to encourage critical-thinking skills and teamwork. Wilderness therapy guides generally work with therapists to develop programs based on individual needs. Guides need to have the people skills necessary to mentor (and control) twelve- to eighteen-year-olds. Wilderness therapist Brad Reedy explains why he thinks wilderness therapy is helpful:

> A lot of what I attribute the success to is what we call primitive living. We provide [the kids with] supplies. We provide them food and all the gear that they need, but they have to do everything themselves every day. They have to build their own shelter. They have to cook their own food. They make fire every day to cook on and stay warm by. They do it in small groups of eight to 10 students. Every lesson you want to impart to them is implicit in daily living.[21]

Do You Need a Degree?

Reedy has a PhD in family therapy, but not all wilderness therapy guides have advanced degrees. However, most wilderness therapy organizations require their adventure guides to have a bachelor of arts degree in wilderness and outdoor therapy or a related field. Adventure tour guides who do not work in the therapy field don't need college degrees to break into the outdoor tourism industry. However, anyone who plans to run his or her own guide business might want to take courses in marketing, management, and business administration—not exactly topics you might imagine studying while tramping through a wilderness area.

Get Certified to Save Lives

While college degrees are optional for most adventure tour guides, several certificates can be extremely helpful for those pursuing a career in outdoor adventure. For example, some states require those who work as mountain guides to be certified in wilderness first aid (WFA). The courses take sixteen hours and are taught over a period of two to three days. Course participants learn to treat musculoskeletal injuries (fractures and broken bones), soft tissue injuries (sprains), heat- and cold-related injuries, and other types of injuries. WFA classes also teach emergency survival skills, making plans for rescues, and what to do during environmental emergencies, such as lightning strikes and avalanches. WFA courses cost around $175, and students receive a WFA certificate upon completion.

The most advanced medical certification goes to wilderness first responders (WFRs), who refer to themselves as "woofers." WFR certification courses teach the principles of wilderness and rescue medicine, cardiopulmonary resuscitation, basic life support, and how to respond to altitude sickness, hypothermia, wounds,

Know Your Stuff

"Let me point out that a good guide knows her/his stuff: the area back roads, fascinating local lore, geology, flora, fauna, best times of day for light or to see wild critters, actively seeks out new & interesting information to share with clients, and most of all (bonus!) is trained in how to save your sorry self if the poop hits the fan (the stuff of which guide nightmares is made of, by the way). So do I love my job? Yes. Do I also work for tips? You bet I do."

—Julie Trevelyan, outdoor journalist

Julie Trevelyan, "10 Things Your Outdoor Guide Will Never Tell You," *Wild Girl Writing* (blog), June 15, 2011. www.wildgirlwriting.com.

An adventure tour guide leads a group on a whitewater rafting trip. To provide safe and enjoyable trips for their clients, guides must have extensive experience and knowledge in a variety of outdoor activities, including hiking, kayaking, backpacking, skiing, and more.

burns, shock, and other afflictions. The focus of woofers is to provide care to patients after an injury occurs and help them survive until an ambulance and paramedics arrive with common medical equipment such as traction splints, backboards, spinal collars, and blood pressure cuffs. (It can take several hours—or even days or weeks—for medical care to arrive in the wilderness, depending on the remoteness of the setting.) A WFR certification course requires seventy-two to eighty hours of classroom training and practice. Graduates of courses take both a written and practical exam. Woofers are usually required by state laws to take recertification courses after two or three years. Woofer Rick Romine explains who benefits from WFR training: "Woofers are usually individuals who are in leadership positions for outdoor adventures such as backpacking, mountain climbing, river rafting, skiing, and similar remote activities. They may be in roles such as trek leader, river guide, or ski patrol. Many reputable outdoor organizations now require Wilderness First Responder certification for all their outdoor employees."[22]

In addition to first-aid skills, prospective guides can enhance their job prospects by taking courses at wilderness institutions like the National Outdoor Leadership School (NOLS), based in Lander, Wyoming. NOLS offers thirty-five-day classes in canoeing, sea and river kayaking, mountain backpacking, rock climbing, and mountaineering. Depending on the subject, the classes are held in the Pacific Northwest, the Rocky Mountains, the Southwest, Alaska, or the Yukon. Graduates of NOLS can pursue work as wilderness guides, outdoor educators, or park rangers.

Those who attend the University of California–Davis can earn college credit while enhancing their guide skills. The school offers one- to two-week courses with names such as Beginning Whitewater Rafting Guide School, Rock Climbing Guide School, and Wilderness Guide School.

While attaining an outdoor education is helpful to those wishing to become adventure tour guides, mountain guide Brett McKay believes that the best way to find employment in the field is to develop a lifelong commitment to outdoor exploration. As McKay explains:

An employable guide candidate will have dedicated himself to his craft, for a number of years, in a recreational fashion. The only way to acquire the minimum fitness, skill, and judgment is to make a life of mountain travel for a period of time. During this time, most will not attend school nor will they work full-time. . . . I did exactly that, deferring "grown-up" life for quite some time. I lived in my car, crashed on couches, worked at ski areas and pizza places and summer camps, all the while learning to ski and climb and manage risk in big, wild mountains.[23]

Low Cost of Living

Those who have dedicated their lives to wilderness exploration can find employment at resorts, parks, lodges, and adventure tourism companies. Some tour guides are self-employed; they find clients on social networks and advertise at sporting goods stores and other outdoor businesses. Others set up their own adventure guide businesses. However, the number of people working as adventure tour guides is very small; there were about ten thousand people working as adventure tour guides throughout the world in 2015. An additional two thousand people were employed as wilderness therapy guides in North America.

Places where adventure tour guide jobs are available are as varied as nature. America's national parks and national forests are magnets for adventurers, and guides can find work in the deserts of Arizona, the mountains of Montana, the Everglades in Florida, and the rain forests of Washington State. Guides can

Guiding Young Adults

"In my job for a wilderness-therapy program, I backpacked through the Southwest deserts with groups of young adults struggling with addiction, behavioral, and psychological issues. They learned practical wilderness skills, but more importantly they grew emotionally and relationally through the power of wilderness. . . . Guides learn leadership skills bringing groups into unfamiliar environments or situations that are outside of clients' skill sets. They are experts in a given wilderness environment, and leaders who keep people safe in perilous places. This kind of job will mold you for the rest of your life."

—Eric Hanson, wilderness therapy guide

Eric Hanson, "10 Reasons: Get a Career in 'Wilderness Industry,'" GearJunkie, July 22, 2016. https://gearjunkie.com.

also go international; numerous ecotourism companies hire adventure guides to take tourists on journeys through environmentally sensitive places in New Zealand, Central and South America, Southeast Asia, and Africa. Knowledge of a foreign language is often required for applicants. Guides are also required to have an understanding of the local environment, as well as knowledge of local culture and religion.

Wherever adventure guides work, they must love adventure and travel more than money. In general, adventure tour guides earn from $50 to $150 a day, depending on their location, experience, type of tour, and training. And adventure clients are expected to tip, which can greatly increase a guide's salary. As one unnamed tour guide explains, "Tips are normally $20 per day as a minimum. . . . The guests will tip you at the end of every day according to how good you were. Customers almost always tip, and this is a great incentive to keep them happy the entire day of the tour. The last tour I worked, I made over $350 in [tips in] just 5 days!"[24]

While the money might not be great, there are benefits to working as an adventure tour guide. Meals, transportation, and accommodations are free to those who work for established tour companies. And adventure tour guides get to work and live in nature's grandeur. Eric Hanson, a field instructor for a wilderness therapy program, describes the benefits of his job: "A low cost of living makes it easy to exist on a modest salary and even save money. Wilderness jobs rarely pay well. But the cost of living while working is very low, with cheap rent and meals covered by your company a possibility with many gigs. A bonus: It can be a great way to pay off debt or save for a big trip."[25]

Find Out More

National Outdoor Leadership School (NOLS)
284 Lincoln St.
Lander, WY 82520
website: www.nols.edu

The NOLS was founded in 1965 to take students on wilderness expeditions and teach them leadership, outdoor skills, and environmental ethics. The school offers a host of courses in outdoor education, wilderness medicine, risk management, and professional guide training.

Professional Association of Wilderness Guides and Instructors (PAWGI)

website: www.pawgi.org

The PAWGI established professional standards for wilderness guides and is a certifying agency for certification programs it developed, including Certified Wilderness Guide and Certified Wilderness Instructor. Anyone interested in becoming an adventure tour guide can enhance their résumé through PAWGI programs.

Wilderness Inquiry

808 Fourteenth Ave. SE
Minneapolis, MN 55414
website: www.wildernessinquiry.org

This organization is dedicated to providing outdoor adventures and universal wilderness access to people of all ages, races, and physical abilities. The website provides information to those seeking employment or volunteer opportunities.

Outdoor Photographer

A Few Facts

Median Salary
$31,710 per year in 2015 for all photographers

Minimum Educational Requirements
High school; a bachelor of arts in photography provides options for advancement

Personal Qualities
Artistic eye, physically fit, knowledge of high-tech photography equipment, software skills, comfortable with financial instability

Working Conditions
Outdoors on photo shoots in all types of weather; indoors when editing and marketing photographs

Number of Jobs
125,000 for all professional photographers in 2015

Job Outlook
About 3 percent growth through 2024

Can you imagine making a living with a camera, taking photographs while hiking through a rain forest, climbing the rock face of a mountain, or diving undersea among coral reefs? For outdoor photographer Andrew Kornylak, this isn't a dream, it's just another day on the job. Kornylak takes photos while hiking, climbing, diving, and other outdoor pursuits. He sells his work to outdoor equipment manufacturers like North Face and to the *Wall Street Journal* and other major media corporations. As the old saying goes, a picture is worth a thousand words, and like all good photographs, Kornylak's tell a compelling story. And as Kornylak explains, one needs to be passionate and completely obsessed with photography to find success. "To be on the road all the time or be in the mountains or whatever, it's kind of all-consuming if you want to do it at a high level,"[26] he says.

It can take a long time to acquire the artistic skills necessary for a career in outdoor photography. Professional outdoor photographers have to develop an artistic eye sensitive to the subtle interplay between line and color, shadows and light. Additionally, they need to understand the rules of good outdoor photography. For example, because most animals are smaller than people, the photographer needs to get down to the eye level of the animal so the viewer can relate to it. Photographers must also have the courage to break the rules when necessary, photographing subjects from odd or interesting angles to highlight their form or actions. The goal is to capture pictures of animals and scenery that elicit emotions in viewers, evoking feelings of happiness, disappointment, anxiety, wonderment, longing, or exhilaration.

While mastering the artistic aspect of shooting photos, a professional outdoor photographer has to understand the complex functions of digital cameras, lenses, lens filters, artificial lighting, memory cards, and exposure meters. Photographers also use complicated image-editing software like Photoshop, Pixelmator, or GIMP in order to manipulate light, shadow, color, and other elements in photographs to improve their appearance.

Freelancing

A good business sense is important to anyone wishing to work as an outdoor photographer. Around 63 percent of all professional photographers are self-employed. While there are no separate figures for outdoor photographers, the number of freelancers in the profession is probably even higher since traditional media, like *National Geographic* and other nature magazines, now rely on freelancers, whereas they once employed photographers full time.

Freelancing has its benefits. The self-employed make their own hours and set their own schedules. And they have more artistic control, since they are not bound by the wants and desires of a boss. However, freelance photographers must pay for their own equipment and office space. They must advertise, set prices, sell their photos, and keep business records. Alistair Blair is a freelance wedding photographer, but his words ring true for outdoor photographers as well. "I learned from a mentor early on that one really needs to be more of a business person than an artist," he maintains. "There are some incredible photographers out

Waiting for Wildlife

"[When shooting in the New Guinea rain forest] I would get in my blind [a shelter] and get set up before it gets light and the birds start arriving around 6:00 a.m. . . . . I'd spend three or four hours in the blind, which is really nothing more than a frame of short poles or a couple of boards lashed between branches . . . surrounded by camouflaged cloth and netting. I get lucky, and the males actually come and display that day and I get some shots, but unfortunately, no females come. I really want to get a female visit, so I'll be back for several more days."

—Tim Laman, wildlife photographer, biologist

Tim Laman, quoted in Mark Edward Harris, "The Wildlife Photojournalist," *Outdoor Photographer*, July 6, 2010. www.outdoorphotographer.com.

there that are eating bread and water, and some really [bad] ones making a fortune! Also, don't start with zero in the bank. Always have a slight financial buffer. Always remember to pay yourself."[27]

Hunting for Images

Millions of people take photos in nature, and many of them are pretty good. And it's safe to say that of the 300 million photos uploaded to Facebook every day, tens of millions feature outdoor and wildlife scenes. With that kind of competition, anyone who wants to earn a living with a camera outdoors has to shoot photos that are much, *much* better than the average vacation snapshot. The mix of shadows and light must be dramatic, the animal behavior rarely seen, and the colors astounding. To attain such pictures, the photographer must be willing to sacrifice. Outdoor photographers leave family and friends behind for weeks at a time to visit the most out-of-the-way places on earth. To financially justify their travel, they often live on a bare-bones budget while sleeping in a tent and eating meals out of cans. Outdoor photographers need

to be fully informed about their surroundings and wildlife subjects, which means spending long hours studying maps and trails, animal behavior websites, and possible problems they might face, such as road closures, wildfires, and severe weather.

Some of the best lighting for photography occurs at dawn, so many outdoor photographers find themselves tramping through the wilderness at 4:00 a.m. waiting to click a unique picture at sunrise. And patience must be learned; animals do not necessarily behave the way a photographer wishes them to, and for every stunning shot of a bird, bear, or butterfly, there are dozens of blurry images of the animals taking off. Weather is another variable; days of heavy overcast, fog, rain, or snow can ruin a trip, leaving the photographer with nothing to show for the effort. While few outdoor photographers would doubt there are negative aspects to the job, taking that one fantastic photo can make up for weeks of fruitless effort.

Learning to Shoot Like a Pro

You don't need a college degree to learn to be an outdoor photographer, but becoming an expert does require shooting thousands of photos—whatever your level of talent or technical skill. As photographer Dan K notes, the influential twentieth-century French photographer Henri Cartier-Bresson famously wrote, "Your first 10,000 photographs are your worst."[28] Cartier-Bresson was implying that it takes endless hours of hands-on practice to learn to use the camera as a storytelling device. Few photographers will dispute his words. Prospective photographers also need to learn to edit their work mercilessly, figuring out which photos work and which ones to delete.

Fledgling photographers do not need to figure everything out on their own. Most communities offer adult education classes that cover technical aspects of photography, equipment, marketing, and software. Basic art courses include principles of photography, image manipulation, and wildlife photography. Business, marketing, and accounting classes with a focus on photography are also available for the self-employed. Those who wish to earn higher wages, working as an environmental photojournalist for example, should think about obtaining a bachelor of arts degree in photography.

Some outdoor photographers at the top of their field have advanced degrees. One example is Tim Laman, whose work often appears in *National Geographic*. Laman has a PhD in biology and uses his training to seek out and photograph rare rain forest animals, such as Borneo orangutans and gnomelike primates called tarsiers. As Laman explains, he uses his photographs to tell strong stories about wildlife: "Shooting wild animals in their environment is really important to me. The animal can't survive without the habitat, and getting the message across in the [photo] of the importance of habitat is critical."[29]

Putting Together a Portfolio

Whatever the educational background, the success of a photographer mainly depends on the quality of his or her portfolio photos. A portfolio was once a large, flat case filled with work that artists used to lug around when seeking employment. Today portfolios are online, which has good points and bad. Obviously, digital portfolios are accessible to anyone online, and they can contain a nearly infinite number of photos. However, a rookie mistake for the prospective outdoor photographer is filling the portfolio with hundreds of pictures that do not have a unifying theme.

A photographic portfolio should consist only of your strongest works, and they should be related to one another. For example, all the photos might be from the Pacific Northwest, or they might all be attention-grabbing shots of birds. The best way to assemble such a portfolio is to start with one hundred photos and edit them down to the best twenty to thirty. Self-editing a photo portfolio can be difficult, since most people have trouble honestly evaluating their own work. Seek input from an impartial person whose judgment you trust, such as a photography teacher or an editor you have worked with.

If you are not an expert at creating websites, you might want to enlist the help of a professional website designer. Either way, the final photos should be tastefully displayed on a website. Links should provide further information, such as thumbnail contact sheets and titles, dates, and locations for each shot. A brief artistic statement is fine, but the blurb should be short and to the point; no long essays on lens settings and atmospheric conditions.

Once you have a great website, you can e-mail the website address (URL) to prospective clients or post it on social media sites. However, if you want to expose your work to the great-

Mixing Art with Business

"Certainly the work needs to be to a certain level of professionalism but then there many other factors that determine success. It's a strange profession in the fact that you need to be equal parts artist and business person. The vast majority of us get into photography from the art perspective for creative reasons, but to make it a sustainable profession we need to understand the business and marketing side of things and it's not very sexy. . . . You have to [be] able to ride out the highs and lows both financially and emotionally. This industry is not for those who need stability."

—Celin Serbo, outdoor photographer

Celin Serbo, quoted in Mike Wilkinson, "Fstoppers Interview with Outdoor Adventure Photographer Celin Serbo," Fstoppers, December 10, 2012. https://fstoppers.com.

est number of people, you need to optimize your website for search engines. Search engine optimization (SEO) is technical and complicated, but what it does is ensure that when someone searches the words "outdoor photographer in (your town)," for example, your website pops up near the top of the list. Essentially, the Google algorithms that determine which links to display are made by a number of factors. For example, an original blog written by you and hosted on your own website helps push your URL to the top of the list. Having certain keywords on your website also helps. There's plenty of SEO information on the web, and it might be worth it to hire someone who specializes in this technical task if the word *optimization* makes your eyelids flutter.

Thinking About Light and Angles

Successful nature photographers spend the better part of their time outdoors, camping, hiking, dealing with weather, and taking photos. An example is provided by Marc Adamus, an award-winning landscape photographer. For the past ten years, Adamus has spent half of every year sleeping in a camper on the back of his pickup truck, parked near sites he wishes to photograph. Like most outdoor photographers, his day begins at 4:00 a.m., when he has a quick breakfast and begins packing his equipment for the day. When taking pictures in the Queets Rainforest in Washington State in 2014, Adamus canoed across rivers and hiked in the pouring rain through dense forests filled with elk and black bears. On this trip, he was planning to get shots of the trees and plants in the rain forest, which include rare 300-foot-high (91-m) old-growth pine trees surrounded by blooming flowers and mushrooms. Adamus describes the shoot: "Every time I spot a possible subject for a photograph, I move very slowly around it, thinking about the light and angles, and trying to analyze in my head where the compositional lines and potential distractions would be. I get out my camera in about one minute and hand-hold many 'test' shots at different positions. . . . I make several 4–6 second exposures of the scene."[30]

An Accessible Career

Adamus is one of the lucky outdoor photographers who can spend his days flexing his artistic muscles while earning a living. And finding success in a Snapchat world of ubiquitous cell phone cameras is increasingly difficult. However, in 2015 around 125,000 people were working as professional photographers; an unknown number worked in the outdoor photography field. Despite the low pay of around $31,710 a year, outdoor photography is an accessible career choice for anyone wishing to invest in classes and camera equipment (considerably cheaper than a college education). And no matter how many photographs make their way onto Facebook, the market for great photos remains strong, since websites need cutting-edge content that only skilled photographers can provide.

Find Out More

Association of International Photography Art Dealers (AIPAD)

2025 M St. NW, Suite 800
Washington, DC 20036
website: www.aipad.com

The AIPAD encourages public support of fine art photography by acting as a voice for the dealers in fine art photography and through communication and education within the photographic community.

North American Nature Photography Association (NANPA)

6382 Charleston Rd.
Alma, IL 62807
website: www.nanpa.org

The NANPA promotes nature photography as a means of communication, nature appreciation, and protection of the environment. The organization publishes informational articles and hosts learning events and webinars. NANPA members in high school and college can apply for scholarships and grants.

Professional Photographers of America (PPA)

229 Peachtree St. NE, Suite 2200
Atlanta, GA 30303

The PPA is the world's largest nonprofit photography association, with more than twenty-nine thousand members in fifty countries. The PPA website offers numerous links to educational resources, networking sources, and certification for professional photographers.

Society for Photographic Education (SPE)

2530 Superior Ave. #403
Cleveland, OH 44114

The SPE promotes an understanding of photography as a means of diverse creative expression, cultural insight, and experimental practice through teaching, learning, scholarship, and criticism.

SOURCE NOTES

Introduction: Air and Sunshine on the Job

1. Eric Hanson, "10 Reasons: Get a Career in 'Wilderness Industry,'" GearJunkie, July 22, 2016. https://gearjunkie.com.
2. Henry David Thoreau, "Walking," *Atlantic*, 2016. www.theatlantic.com.
3. John Muir, "9 John Muir Quotes to Live By," *The Clymb* (blog), 2016. http://blog.theclymb.com.

Farmer

4. Keith Jolley, "Mathline," PBS, 2015. www.pbs.org.
5. Quoted in Brian K. Marbry, "USDA Invests $18 Million to Train Beginning Farmers and Ranchers," US Department of Agriuclture, February 2, 2015. www.usda.gov.
6. Jesse Hirsch, "So You Want to Be a Farmer. . . ," *Modern Farmer*, September 15, 2014. http://modernfarmer.com.

Marine Biologist

7. Milton Love, "So You Want to Be a Marine Biologist? The Revenge!," Love Lab, 2015. www.lovelab.id.ucsb.edu.
8. Love, "So You Want to Be a Marine Biologist? The Revenge!"
9. Quoted in Michael Bear, "Interview with Richard Wylie, Marine Biologist," *Marine Science Today*, June 13, 2013. http://marinesciencetoday.com.
10. Quoted in Bear, "Interview with Richard Wylie, Marine Biologist."

Park Ranger

11. Andrea Lankford, "Ranger Confidential: Secrets of the National Park Rangers," Backpacker, September 2010. www.backpacker.com.

12. Rocky, "How to Land a Park Ranger Job," *The Clymb* (blog), 2016. http://blog.theclymb.com.
13. Rocky, "How to Land a Park Ranger Job."
14. Nathan Rott, "Life in the Park: Finding Meaning in Park Service Work," NPR, July 21, 2016. www.npr.org.
15. Stacy Czebotar, "Reflections of a Former Park Ranger," Washington Trails Association, April 2012. www.wta.org.

Wildland Firefighter

16. US Forest Service, *So You Want to Be a . . . Wildland Firefighter*, 2016. www.fs.usda.gov.
17. Drew Miller, "5 Ways Wildfire Fighting Is Exactly as Insane as It Sounds," Cracked, March 25, 2014. www.cracked.com.

Horticulturist

18. Crystal, "Career Day: Horticulturist," Aspiring Mormon Women, January 24, 2014. http://aspiringmormonwomen.org.
19. Elise Newman, "An Insider's Look at the Horticultural Department: Part 1," San Diego Zoo Global *ZooNooz*, March 12, 2015. http://zoonooz.sandiegozoo.org.

Adventure Tour Guide

20. Julie Trevelyan, "10 Things Your Outdoor Guide Will Never Tell You," *Wild Girl Writing* (blog), June 15, 2011. www.wildgirlwriting.com.
21. Quoted in Noah Davis, "How They Got There: A Conversation with Wilderness Therapist Brad Reedy," Awl, March 26, 2012. https://theawl.com.
22. Rick Romine, "How to Become a Certified Wilderness First Responder (WFR)," HowToWilderness.com, January 27, 2012. http://howtowilderness.com.
23. Brett McKay and Kate McKay, "So You Want My Job: Mountain Guide," *Art of Manliness*, March 22, 2013. www.artofmanliness.com.
24. Quoted in Job Monkey, "Tour Guide Pay and Benefits," 2016. www.jobmonkey.com.
25. Hanson, "10 Reasons."

Outdoor Photographer

26. Quoted in Jeff Kinney, "Living the Dream: Top 10 Best Outdoor Jobs," Blue Ridge Outdoors, April 16, 2015. www.blueridgeoutdoors.com.
27. Quoted in Lauren Margolis, "11 Things Photographers Wish They Knew Before Going Freelance," *Photoshelter Blog*, July 29, 2013. http://blog.photoshelter.com.
28. Quoted in Dan K, "Your First 10,000 Photographs May Include Some of Your Best," PetaPixel, June 11, 2013. http://petapixel.com.
29. Quoted in Mark Edward Harris, "The Wildlife Photojournalist," *Outdoor Photographer*, July 6, 2010. www.outdoorphotographer.com.
30. Quoted in Klassy Goldberg, "A Day in the Life of Landscape Photographer Marc Adamus," 500PX, 2014. https://iso.500px.com.

INTERVIEW WITH A HORTICULTURIST

Roy Wilburn is horticulture manager at Sunshine Care, an assisted-living facility in Poway, California. In this job, which he has held since 2010, he oversees a greenhouse and five organic gardens that produce fruits and vegetables for the facility's residents. He is responsible for all landscaping at the 32-acre property and runs gardening programs for children and horticultural therapy programs for Sunshine Care's residents. Before coming to Sunshine Care, he spent twenty years as a farm owner, grower, and manager in Baja California, Mexico. He has also worked as a grower and manager of an herb farm in Oceanside, California. He answered these interview questions via e-mail.

Q: Why did you become a horticulturist?

A: My college girlfriend's father was looking for someone with a math and science background (I had math degree and a marine biology minor) to mold as his assistant. He was a tomato grower in Baja, California. I loved the life on the coast of Baja and enjoyed the outdoors. I accepted the job and ended up marrying the farmer's daughter.

Q: Can you describe your training?

A: I was thrown into a tomato field and didn't see my boss for three weeks. So I didn't have any real training for this job but I knew what I had to do and my role to make us a success. I made valuable contacts with the local universities, seed and chemical companies, irrigation suppliers and got to travel the world studying different agricultural innovations to keep up on the cutting edge of a highly competitive business.

Q: Can you describe your typical workday?

A: After coming in early, around 4 a.m., I answer e-mails, write blogs, attack paperwork and all the other boring stuff. When the sun starts to rise or before, I go to the greenhouse and check on all the seedlings for the gardens. I then prepare for the arrival of my special needs groups or prepare for the day's horticultural therapy sessions with our residents. (In these sessions we get our residents active in the gardens or greenhouse. They might do something like flower arranging or they might plant or repot or harvest plants.) Then off I go to the gardens to plant, harvest, and check for diseases and insect damage on the crops that are growing. At that time I also get together with my worker to lay out his workday usually tackling some landscaping duty. Before I leave, I say "good night" to my babies in the greenhouse.

Q: What would you say is the biggest challenge you have faced in your job?

A: I had no previous experience with roses, succulents, trees, flowers in general and other landscape material prior to working here at Sunshine Care. I was well-versed in growing fruits and vegetables commercially but had to adjust to growing produce organically. I had to take classes, meet people, ask questions, and get out there and kill a few plants before I got the experience to grow them successfully. It's all part of horticulture. Working with irrigation problems during our drought conditions and water restrictions has been a huge challenge.

Q: What do you like most about your job?

A: We have a children's garden for the benefit of local home-schooled children and preschoolers. They work in the garden, planting and harvesting. As part of our Seed-to-Table Intergenerational Program, the kids and residents work together in the greenhouse. The smiles on the residents' faces are priceless! Educating children about the world of horticulture is extremely important. It's especially important that they witness firsthand where their food comes from. Children who work in gardens end up eating five times the amount of fresh fruits and vegetables than those that don't. I love growing little gardeners!

Q: Can you describe something about your job that is especially rewarding?

A: Watching children pull a cherry tomato off a plant or pull a carrot out of the ground, then eating it with zeal makes me very happy. Meeting up with someone on the street and hearing them say that the vegetable plant I gave them yielded something delicious for their family to enjoy also gets me excited.

Q: What do you like least about your job?

A: Don't really enjoy weeding in 100-degree weather but it is still therapeutic, necessary, and still beats working indoors.

Q: What personal qualities do you find most valuable for this type of work?

A: It helps to be outgoing and easygoing. Showing compassion to the elderly and being a good helpful example to future generations of gardeners is vital.

Q: What advice do you have for students who might be interested in a career as a horticulturist?

A: Drop your cell phones and iPads for a while and get outside and experience nature at its finest. Get your hands dirty and study hard! Get out there and volunteer in your community.

Q: How important is the love of working outdoors to your career?

A: This is imperative in my situation!! I am almost always outdoors and growing plants is where this all happens unless you work in a greenhouse situation. You have to love what you do otherwise it is just work.

OTHER CAREERS IF YOU LIKE THE OUTDOORS

Agricultural equipment
  technician
Agronomist
Animal trainer
Arborist
Archaeologist
Beekeeper
Boat captain
Cartographer
Construction worker
Environmental scientist
Explosives technician
Fisher
Fish farmer
Forester
Gamekeeper
Geologist
Groundskeeper
Horse riding instructor
Irrigation technician
Kennel worker
Landscape architect

Land surveyor
Logger
Meteorologist
Mining engineer
Natural resource manager
Ornithologist
Outdoor educator
Pest management
  technician
Petroleum engineer
Rancher
Resort manager
Seismologist
Ski instructor
Travel guide
Urban planner
Veterinarian
Vineyard manager
Volcanologist
Wildlife conservationist
Wind turbine engineer
Zoologist

Editor's note: The online *Occupational Outlook Handbook* of the US Department of Labor's Bureau of Labor Statistics is an excellent source of information on jobs in hundreds of career fields, including many of those listed here. The *Occupational Outlook Handbook* may be accessed online at www.bls.gov/ooh.

INDEX

Note: Boldface page numbers indicate illustrations.

PICTURE CREDITS

ABOUT THE AUTHOR

Stuart A. Kallen is the author of more than 350 nonfiction books for children and young adults. He has written on topics ranging from the theory of relativity to the art of electronic dance music. In addition, Kallen has written award-winning children's videos and television scripts. In his spare time he is a singer, songwriter, and guitarist in San Diego.